FOR

I THINK YOU'D ENJOY THIS BOOK BECAUSE

FROM

PRINCIPLES FOR THE NEXT CENTURY OF WORK

Sense & Respond Press publishes short, beautiful, actionable books on topics related to innovation, digital transformation, product management, and design. Our readers are smart, busy, practical innovators. Our authors are experts working in the fields they write about.

The goal of every book in our series is to solve a real-world problem for our readers. Whether that be understanding a complex and emerging topic, or something as concrete (and difficult) as hiring innovation leaders, our books help working professionals get better at their jobs, quickly.

Jeff Gothelf & Josh Seiden

Series co-editors **Jeff Gothelf** and **Josh Seiden** wrote *Lean UX* (O'Reilly) and *Sense & Respond* (Harvard Business Review Press) together. They were co-founding principals of Neo Innovation (sold to Pivotal Labs) in New York City and helped build it into one of the most recognized brands in modern product strategy, development, and design. In 2017 they were short-listed for the Thinkers50 award for their contributions to innovation leadership. Learn more about Jeff and Josh at www.jeffgothelf.com and www.joshseiden.com.

OTHER BOOKS FROM SENSE & RESPOND PRESS

Lean vs. Agile vs. Design Thinking
*What you really need to know to build
high-performing digital product teams*
Jeff Gothelf

Making Progress
The 7 responsibilities of the innovation leader
Ryan Jacoby

Hire Women
An Agile framework for hiring and retaining women in technology
Debbie Madden

Hiring for the Innovation Economy
Three steps to improve performance and diversity
Nicole Rufuku

Lateral Leadership
A practical guide for agile product managers
Tim Herbig

The Invisible Leader
*Facilitation secrets for catalyzing change,
cultivating innovation, and commanding results*
Elena Astilleros

The Government Fix
How to innovate in government
Hana Schank & Sara Hudson

Outcomes Over Output
Why customer behavior is the key metric for business success
Josh Seiden

What CEOs Need to Know About Design
A business leader's guide to working with designers
Audrey Crane

OKRs at the Center
How to use goals to drive ongoing change and create the organization you want
Natalija Hellesoe & Sonja Mewes

To keep up with new releases or submit book ideas to the press, check out our website at www.senseandrespondpress.com.

ETHICAL PRODUCT DEVELOPMENT

Copyright © 2020 by Pavani Reddy

All rights reserved. No part of this publication may be reproduced, stored in a retrieval system, or transmitted, in any form or by any means, electronic, mechanical, photocopying, recording, or otherwise, without the prior written permission of the publisher.

Issued in print and electronic formats.

ISBN 979-8-6662990-4-3 (paperback).

Designer: Mimi O Chun
Interior typesetting: Jennifer Blais

Published in the United States by Sense & Respond Press, www.senseandrespondpress.com

Printed and bound in the United States.
1 2 3 4   23 22 21 20

Pavani Reddy

ETHICAL PRODUCT DEVELOPMENT

Practical techniques to apply across the product development life cycle

INTRODUCTION

When I told my friend and former colleague that I was writing a practical book about ethical product development, she said: "That's great news because I feel like I'm in a dystopia."

Though she lives in Silicon Valley and works in technology, my friend does not work at Facebook, Google, Amazon, Twitter, or any of the other high-profile companies that routinely contend with public controversies. Yet she—and nearly every other product professional I know—confronts ethical questions every day. My friend was referring to the dystopia created by people who work in technology who make all sorts of decisions without a good handle on their ethical ramifications. This conversation took place in January 2020, a couple of months before the global novel coronavirus pandemic took center stage closely followed by global acknowledgement of the longstanding crisis of racial injustice in the United States and around the world, brought back into public consciousness by the horrific murder of George Floyd by police on May 25 in Minneapolis, Minnesota. By the time this book is in your hands, we will all live in a chapter called "after the pandemic first hit," when even more questions will arise as to the impact of our technology products.

In March 2020, as hundreds of millions of additional people began using Zoom video conferencing to connect with coworkers, friends, and family during this time of widespread physical distancing, Zoom found itself in a spotty spotlight. Zoom's massive growth was curbed by what many people considered serious oversights in privacy and security, which included allowing bad actors to hack easily into meetings. The company claimed to have a type of secure encryption that its software did not have. Some of Zoom's other oversights involved mistakenly routing video calls through China as well as sending user data to Facebook—even the data of non-Facebook users. New York City's Department of Education, Google, SpaceX, Twitter, and droves of other companies initially banned Zoom's use, while Zoom pursued a three-month "new feature freeze" to address these concerns.

Zoom's oversights were costly. They forced Zoom to play three months of catch-up during what could have been the company's golden opportunity to beat nearly all their competitors. Zoom now must address lawsuits like one brought by a San Francisco church whose Bible study class was infiltrated by a hacker who bombarded the video call with child pornography. "[We] recognize that we have fallen short of the community's—and our own—privacy and security expectations," wrote Eric Yuan, Zoom's CEO, apologizing in a blog post. "The risks, the misuse, we never thought about that," he said. He explained how the company had been more focused on business enterprise users than on consumer users.

As I watch all of this unfold, I think back to Zoom meetings I had with Yuan himself in 2013, as a Zoom beta user. I recall his enthusiasm for the software and passion for ensuring that it met our needs. Much to my team's delight, the Zoom staff took our input along with that of other beta customers and rolled out updates, quickly. And I think about the rest of us who work on technology, who operate so similarly to Yuan and his colleagues. Most of us involved in product development also face questions of how to handle and use people's personal information. Safeguard it? Sell it to other businesses? Share it with the government? Use it to market adjacent products and services? Use it to nudge behavior? Feed it to machine learning tools? To what end? How do we collect user consent? Do we proceed with the same kinds of plans post-pandemic? These weighty questions intertwine with seemingly mundane ones, leaving us making myriad ethical choices in haphazard or unintentional ways, perhaps just like they were made at Zoom.

And in the last few years, those of us that follow tech news have observed a familiar cycle of delayed reaction to ethical shortcomings, the headlines themselves becoming non-news of sorts.

Racism finds its way into home-sharing and ride-sharing platforms. Search platforms show ads for higher paying jobs to more men than women. Teens now experience unprecedented levels of anxiety, addiction, and self-harm as they use online social networking platforms. In response to the headlines, we often see formal retractions of features or changes in user policies. As part of the cycle, in some instances, a product leader writes a "regreditorial" or the tech media analyzes the situation in a case study.

We come up with a variety of root causes of these harmful product consequences. Sometimes we conclude that no one could have reasonably foreseen the harm. Other times, we think bad ethics happen to bad people or bad business models. Still other times, we think regulation has fallen too far behind. Many of us also lament the lack of all kinds of diversity in the tech sector. These root causes often do have some truth to them and should be addressed. But as a sector, we've glossed over a major flaw in the whole approach: the absence of ethical decision-making at every important juncture of the product development process.

Though most of us do not consciously set aside ethics, the product development approach that we use today omits ethical analysis and—in some respects—even *avoids* it. The ethical decision points we regularly encounter come and go. Most of the time, we ignore the non-egregious, yet harmful, consequences of our decisions or lack of decisions. When the consequences become tough to ignore because they are so bad or we are called out due to our size or some other reason, only then do we react.

While I am concerned about the unfortunate impact of many, everyday technologies, I am equally concerned that as a sector and as technology workers, we do not routinely discuss—in a practical way—how to go about producing ethical products in the first place. Proposals to improve the ethical impact of technologies range from bringing about regulation in the technology sector to mandating professional licensure for various roles, such as product managers, designers, software engineers, and data scientists, akin to how other professions seek to standardize ethics through licensing. Still other suggestions involve getting more serious about improving diversity, equity, and inclusion in the field. While the details of these possible solutions make all the difference as to whether or not they are good ideas, the main problem with them all: They are long-term solutions and removed from the day-to-day of product development.

Noting this gap, I've written what I hope is a user-friendly guide on steps product developers could take to produce ethical products. Why? Because I have faith in us to take more proactive steps to address ethical shortcomings and—better yet—to avoid them in the first place. By incorporating the techniques in this book directly into the product development process, we as product leaders can begin to break the cycle. We can plan more ethical products and manage their ethical trajectory. And we should. Not only to minimize risk, but also to serve society. To borrow a construct from President Kennedy, as product leaders, we would do this not because it is easy but because building ethical products is hard. Careful consideration is required.

My years executing the process have revealed to me five key imperatives for product leaders. I break down the "why" and "how" of each of these imperatives into five chapters and 20 practical techniques, listed as Takeaways at the end of each chapter. The five key imperatives:

1. Build a product code of ethics as a foundation for your product.

2. Establish a champion for each element of the code of ethics.

3. Identify the product's ethical failures—what I call the "ethical floor."

4. Bake ethics into your existing product development process.

5. Build in opportunities to strengthen your own personal ethics.

My bold assertion in this book is that investing in ethical product development is not only desirable, but also practical and cost effective. I see this investment as inseparable from investing in innovation and the long-term success of the product itself. Jim Collins, in *Good to Great*, famously shows that companies that invest in purpose beyond profits return more value to shareholders over the long term. Many other studies since then demonstrate the same. Jonathan Haidt, a business ethics professor at New York University, confirms that companies with a solid reputation command higher prices, pay less for capital, and land better talent, while companies caught in ethical lapses struggle with these dimensions for years. Though tougher to measure, Haidt points out that companies that incorporate ethics operate more efficiently based on the way employees approach their work for reasons likely having to do with motivation, purpose, and loyalty.

This research may be enough to convince you that the case for investing in an ethical product development process exists; but if you are not convinced or can cite too many counterexamples, shift the frame slightly to ask whether the economic case changes if companies incurred virtually no additional costs by following a process that seamlessly incorporates ethics? This book offers you a blueprint for how to upgrade the process you have today, to make ethical consideration inseparable from the approach you take to develop products in the first place.

I believe in the compounding power of each of us who works on technology products for human beings and humanity to incorporate ethical decision-making every step of the way. I'm under no illusion that this process will bring about a tech-centered utopia, but we who use the process can imagine, build, and iterate toward a better future.

CHAPTER 1: ARTICULATE YOUR ASPIRATIONS WITH A PRODUCT CODE OF ETHICS

A Product Code of Ethics (PCOE) is a set of two to 12 principles that a team establishes to help themselves make decisions about how best to serve users and society at large with the product. Written in the manner of guidelines for conduct, each principle articulates a goal or aspiration, such as "avoid creating or reinforcing unfair bias."

The benefit of a PCOE is that it can serve as a navigation device to help your organization make many decisions about how to build and evolve your product. You can apply these principles to make large and small choices. For example, when you have a PCOE, you can more easily target customers and partners who share in the values underlying your principles. Developing your product without a PCOE is like developing it without a product strategy: If you don't know where you are going from an ethics standpoint, how do you get there effectively and, even more importantly, avoid getting totally lost?

A PCOE IN PRACTICE

Let's dive into one of the most widely recognized PCOEs, Google's artificial intelligence (AI) principles, and a brief history of its evolution.

In Google's early years, engineers, wanting to cut through the fluff of corporate value statements, articulated a motto: "Don't be evil." The slogan endured for over 15 years. In 2015, Alphabet, Google's parent, replaced the phrase with "Do the right thing," finally acknowledging the concerns of people who disliked the bar being set at merely avoiding bad behavior and those who deemed some of the company's practices as not living up to the value. "Do the right thing" became part of the larger parent company's code of conduct, no longer specific to the way the search team aimed to develop the product. In June 2018, after controversy over Google's participation in a Department of Defense drone project, Google published AI principles to guide its work in this arena. The first principle in it: "Be socially beneficial."

Once the team had this PCOE in place, the team applied the principle to decide to forgo renewing the controversial $10 billion drone project. A Google representative said, if these AI principles had been available earlier, they likely would've helped the team to decide *not* to become involved in the controversial Pentagon drone project in the first place.

"Do the right thing" did not quite translate into helping Google's AI team decide whether to use AI for military purposes. That principle was too broad, which is often the case with the values expressed in corporate values statements or general codes of conduct. Yet most companies rely on these alone, rather than developing a PCOE for each major product. Companies that do take the step to develop a PCOE and use it regularly to make decisions give themselves a vast vocabulary to pursue aspirational goals more deliberately.

Google's AI Principles and Application:

» *"Be socially beneficial"*:
 Google proceeds with projects in which the company believes that the overall intended benefits of AI substantially exceed the foreseeable risks and downsides."

» *"Avoid creating or reinforcing unfair bias"*:
 Google recognizes that distinguishing between fair and unfair bias is complex across cultures, but also calls out a clear aim to avoid "unjust impacts" on people who have "sensitive characteristics" such as "race, ethnicity, gender, nationality, income, sexual orientation, and political or religious belief."

» *"Be built and tested for safety"*:
 Google has established deep research programs that highlight possible categorical AI failures and ways to test for these failures.

» *"Be accountable to people"*:
 Google has built teams and processes to evaluate AI

from multiple perspectives ranging from scientific to legal to social.
- » *"Incorporate privacy design principles"*: Google references a separate set of privacy principles to safeguard user data directly as well as to enable users to protect themselves from inappropriate use of their data.
- » *"Uphold standards of scientific excellence"*: Google looks to scientific domain experts and shares findings with the wider AI ecosystem.

DEVELOP YOUR PCOE WITH THE "ETHICS EIGHT" QUESTION FRAMEWORK

How do you create a PCOE? Most companies, including yours, can start the process of establishing your PCOE by referring to your company's statement of values or general code of conduct, if these have been articulated as part of the brand. You have the option to start here instead of on a blank screen or sheet of paper. You can then draft a more specific PCOE to clarify the commitments your company will make to your users and broader society.

Whether you are creating your PCOE from scratch or refining a set of principles that already exist, you should use this eight-question framework—the Ethics Eight—to clarify your principles. Most of the publicly available PCOEs we see, including Google's AI principles, answer these questions. These questions can help your team surface ethical issues embedded in the product you aspire to deliver.

1. **Problems:** What problem(s) do we aim to solve with the product? For whom? How are we doing this in a unique way? And how will we measure outcomes?

2. **Users:** Among users, who is vulnerable? Who is powerful? Who are we leaving out that we do not intend to leave out?

3. **Intended Use:** What does intended use of our product look like? Extreme use? Scaled use? Incomplete use?

4. **Unintended Use:** What are negative side effects or consequences of intended use by intended users? Of unintended uses? Of unintended users? Of both? What are the consequences of use by bad actors? Of negative use cases?

5. **Risk:** How will we disclose risks to our users? How will we get their input on the decisions we are making?

6. **Testing:** How will we quality test our product holistically, i.e., not only from an efficacy standpoint but also from an ethical standpoint? How will we pursue testing itself in an unbiased way?

7. **Broader Impact:** What are negative side effects of usage on non-users/broader stakeholders/society?

8. **Upholding Principles:** How will we help different people on our product team, across the company, and outside of the company uphold and evolve the principles we develop?
   a. Which domain experts should we consult?
   b. What are the current applicable legal regulations? Is the regulatory landscape changing and how will we stay abreast of changes?

c. What types of policies do our peers or competitors with similar products appear to follow?

Note that I started with problems-to-be-solved for our users and ended with the law and competitors in that order, to encourage the team to envision a true north and then match that with the current environment. Like we tell grade-schoolers: Just because someone else is doing something, doesn't make it the right thing to do. Also, just because the product currently operates above the legal threshold—or there is no legal threshold—does not mean that one is not on its way or that a deep inquiry into the other areas is unwarranted.

DRAFTING YOUR PCOE

To develop a draft of your PCOE, enlist a team to brainstorm answers to the Ethics Eight for your product. The goal of this team is to evolve a PCOE that stands up to public scrutiny. This team will participate in four distinct sessions to evolve the PCOE for four audiences, providing each audience a robust opportunity to give input and evaluate how that input has been incorporated. This four-step journey of developing the PCOE can also be turned into a series of blog posts, for internal audiences—and, if appropriate, for external audiences as well.

At this stage, it is useful to dive into the distinction between rules, standards, and principles to illustrate that it is typically most feasible to express your PCOE in the form of principles. As an example:

- » *Rule:* The president of our country must be at least 35 years of age.
- » *Standard:* The president must be an adult.
- » *Principle:* The president must be emotionally mature.

Without diving deep into the pros and cons of policymaking through rules versus standards versus principles, you can see that a principle expresses an aspiration to aid in decision-making. It expresses the spirit of what your team is aiming to do, even when the ideal is not fully defined or definable. If the law has provided bright line rules already, these can be referenced as the minimum.

Consider a four-session approach to working through the Ethics Eight:

SESSION 1
Answer the Ethics Eight to articulate the basics.

Deliverable
First draft of PCOE, consists of two to 12 principles

Target Audience (and where to post the Deliverable)
Product team (in your team space)

Ask Your Audience
How is the team, using PCOE to help make/debate decisions?

SESSION 2
Discuss how the PCOE is being used to make or influence decisions; refine your draft by amplifying principles that the team finds useful to decision-making.

Deliverable
Second draft, incorporates how PCOE has been used to make or influence decisions

Target Audience (and where to post the Deliverable)
Product team and broader company
(on your internal website)

Ask Your Audience
Do the aspirations in the PCOE align with the company's broader positioning?

SESSION 3
Discuss the PCOE's alignment or dissonance with the broader company; resolve dissonance.

Deliverable
Third draft, aligns with the company's other expressed values

Target Audience (and where to post the Deliverable)
Product advisory council
(through a meeting or webinar)

Ask Your Audience
Does the PCOE inspire confidence?

SESSION 4
Discuss customer perception of the PCOE; amplify what's important to your customers.

Deliverable
Fourth draft, calibrates customer concern

Target Audience (and where to post the Deliverable)
Broad market (on your external website)

Ask Your Audience
Does the PCOE resonate with prospective customers, employees, and the broader community?

For those of you who may be concerned with introducing yet another priority, the exercise need not be hugely time-consuming. The first step can be as lightweight as identifying a pair of people who excel at gathering and articulating group input. They can set aside just four hours across an entire year to iterate on the PCOE and still have the exercise yield large benefits. Companies who have created their PCOEs share that the value derived for the time spent has been huge, especially on metrics around employee engagement.

TAKEAWAY FROM THIS CHAPTER
» **Technique 1 of 20.** Write a Product Code of Ethics (PCOE) to guide your work. Recognize that its power will be not only in its existence but also in how it is applied to decision-making.

In the Reading List at the end of this book, I've provided a list of additional resources for each corresponding Takeaway. Taken together these takeaways provide a list of 20 specific actions you can take to build ethics into your product development process.

CHAPTER 2: ANIMATE YOUR PCOE BY ESTABLISHING PRINCIPLE CHAMPIONS

After the publication of Google's AI principles, Kent Walker, senior vice president of global affairs, outlined in a blog post how the company routinely applies the AI principles to their projects. Three core groups at Google apply its seven AI principles to assess new projects, products, and deals through the prism of the principles.

These groups include the cross-functional product team as well as a group of senior "principle" experts from each discipline and a broader council of senior executives across Alphabet (Google's parent company). In addition to using the AI principles to help teams make decisions, Google employees use them to source relevant training and conduct research that deepens their commitment to the principles. Teams at Google report on these efforts publicly. To achieve similar results in transparency, you will need to enlist "principle champions" to bring your PCOE to life.

IDENTIFY PCOE PRINCIPLE CHAMPIONS

To elevate PCOE adherence to the C-suite, in early 2019, Salesforce appointed Paula Goldman to be its first-ever chief ethical and humane use officer. Goldman took this role after having served on the company's advisory council, consisting of Salesforce employees and external technology experts. While having an executive role of this nature would provide unique opportunities, it need not be the starting point. The starting point can be as simple as identifying colleagues as principle champions. In a similar model, many organizations follow a process for employees to nominate their colleagues as culture champions, or champions of company values; some also create similar matching awards for their customers who espouse these values.

Your PCOE drafting process from Chapter 1 can lend itself nicely to identifying champions who can then create a community and follow a playbook to uphold the principles. Strong candidates for the voluntary post include individuals on the product development team who show enthusiasm for drafting the PCOE as well as leaders across the company who contribute productively to evolving it. It is helpful to match champions with a distinct principle or small collection of principles based on their unique interest in an area, so that they can build their depth of knowledge and perspective in the area. Passion for the principle(s) is an important criterion for selection, but perhaps even more important is each principle champion's ability to engage in productive dialogue with people who have alternate viewpoints. This will be essential to running the Principle Playbook.

RUN THE PRINCIPLE PLAYBOOK

Once you identify the PCOE principle champions, these champions can follow a principle playbook that allows them to uphold and evolve each principle in collaboration with the product development team. This playbook consists of six principle-specific activities.

ACTIVITY 1
Develop a risk-zone framework.

As Salesforce's chief ethical and humane use officer, one of Goldman's priorities is to work across product leadership to formalize an ethical risk-zone framework. A risk-zone framework tracks the existing and emerging categories of risk related to each aspirational principle in the PCOE. Like Goldman, each principle champion can begin to deepen their understanding of the risk zones relevant to their principle. You might consider adapting a toolkit such as Ethical OS, which contains checklists and scenarios for different types of risk zones, such as "economic and asset inequalities" or "machine learning and algorithmic bias" or "implicit trust and user understanding." The champion can then provide colleagues some future-proofing strategies, such as "red flag rules," a list of social and ethical "red flags" to detect, report, and address.

ACTIVITY 2
Audit the product by principle.
Chapter 3 provides techniques to identify ethical debt in your product. As a principle champion, you will want to supplement the overall audit by building a backlog of principle-specific ethical debt and tracking the backlog.

ACTIVITY 3
Source and deploy principle-specific expert training.
Identify current experts and best-in-breed training. For example, the champion of the principle to "avoid creating or reinforcing unfair bias" can identify industry experts and source bias training. The champion of privacy can source privacy experts in your sector as well as tailored privacy training.

ACTIVITY 4
Learn how to discuss ethical options when making product decisions.
First, all principle champions must undergo some form of contemporary open-mindedness training. Reasonable, ethical people can and will disagree about ethical options. But how do you ask good questions about the different perspectives that people will inevitably bring to the table? I recommend OpenMind, an interactive platform launched by Jonathan Haidt, a business ethics professor at NYU, to help individuals and teams understand the perspectives of others, learn and grow from challenging conversations, and speak constructively across differences.

Clarifying vocabulary allows people to discuss values and principles in the workplace: values being beliefs, attitudes, and opinions that people hold regarding specific issues. Though values can be shared, they are subjective, can conflict with one another, and can change over time. As we discussed, principles, in contrast, are more like instructions for conduct that lead to an effect. For example, the Google principle "to avoid creating or reinforcing unfair bias" would result in an effect of less "unfair bias," which reflects an underlying value like "equity" and "care for others."

The most user-friendly ethics vocabulary I've found to bring into the throes of the software development process is the Markkula Center's Framework for Ethical Decision-Making. The Markkula Center for Applied Ethics at Santa Clara University, in Silicon Valley, unpacks five classic ethics approaches to help regular people (i.e., those who have not studied philosophy) consider ethical options as we use new technology to solve problems. The approaches are applicable to technology decision-making and are used by companies across Silicon Valley, including Google. They can be used to inform your PCOE as well as to help your team make everyday decisions that should be informed by your PCOE once you have it in place. For more details on how to use the Markkula Framework, see Reading List.

ACTIVITY 5
Help colleagues use the PCOE early and often.

In Chapter 4, I discuss how your product development team can leverage the PCOE in the development process. The principle champions can consider additional ways to elevate the PCOE into the types of metrics that your company monitors, the senior management and investor meetings the company undertakes, and how team members are reviewed on a regular basis for their performance. One suggestion: Host a half-day PCOE event, perhaps in conjunction with a hackathon or set of innovation days that you may have in place, to explore the principles more extensively. In addition to having your PCOE champions examine how your product fares from an ethical standpoint and deploy training, you might consider inviting external experts and customers to join the team to discuss a PCOE principle in play. This ongoing work will ultimately embed the PCOE into your company's DNA.

ACTIVITY 6
Refresh the PCOE.

Principle champions should convene to refresh the PCOE regularly, at least annually, to ensure relevance. In the refresh process, ensure that the mission of the product continues to align well with the mission of the company, as expressed in other collateral. This may mean that one or the other needs adjustment. When the PCOE stays true to the company's expressed mission, you can create a virtuous cycle, gaining internal and external supporters at every rotation. The PCOE helps move the mission forward; in turn, the company's mission supports the team in upholding the PCOE.

As you update it, continue to strive to express your PCOE as simply as possible. At any given point, the PCOE should have no more than 12 principles that can be well understood by those who work inside the company as well as the general public. If there is a need to expand beyond a dozen, consider elaboration under a digestible number of umbrella principles or consider separating out aspects of your product, such as AI or universal design into their own areas with associated PCOEs.

TAKEAWAY FROM THIS CHAPTER

» **Technique 2 of 20.** Identify a champion for each of the PCOE principles, based on your colleagues' interest, expertise, and ability to engage with alternative points of view. Provide the champions with a playbook of activities to help the organization absorb, apply, and evolve the principles.

CHAPTER 3: IDENTIFY THE ETHICAL SHORTCOMINGS OF YOUR PRODUCT TODAY

Once you've established your PCOE, which is aspirational, and identified principle champions to advance these aspirations, it's important to find your product's ethical floor—your current reality. Once you've found the floor, you can start the systematic process of raising it. Correcting bad precedent is an important step in improving the ethics of your product. Use this chapter to identify a few areas you plan to address.

ETHICAL PRODUCT DEVELOPMENT

Mike Davidson, known for building a 100-person design and research team at Twitter, explains in a blog post how "ethical anchoring" occurs. His take will likely ring true to you, as it has to my peers across several different technology companies. Davidson describes how a seemingly small decision, such as defaulting to adding a product warranty into a user's shopping cart to increase the order's cost, establishes a dark pattern. Down the road, when employees want to use more dark patterns, here is how the conversation would go:

> Greg: "Hey, we aren't getting enough people to opt into our mailing list when they sign up. Can we try maybe unchecking that box by default but using language such that leaving it unchecked opts people in?"
>
> Desi: "Wouldn't we be intentionally deceiving users if we did that?"
>
> Greg: "Uhhhh, we already add things to your shopping cart that you don't even ask for!"
>
> Desi: "True. This seems like less of a big deal than that. I guess I'm OK with it."

This conversation illustrates how precedent, or prior decisions, govern future decision-making. Davidson points out that using precedent is not only a low-effort way to inform your current decision, but also "an easy way to cover your ass." In the above scenario, if questioned about her decision-making, the product manager "needs only to point to the shopping cart behavior in order to let herself off the hook."

This chapter follows the chapters on implementing a PCOE because it is essential to view the product's aspirations—what the product wants to be—alongside decisions that the team has made along the way: what the product currently does. Product teams look to both the principles and the precedent. Thus, this chapter is all about evaluating precedents in order to identify the ethical floor and raise that floor by understanding the worst few precedents in your product's ethical trajectory that require a closer analysis.

TECHNIQUE 3
Use Personas to Identify Who You Are Under-serving
One way to use personas to find the ethical floor in your product—particularly to learn who it does not serve—is to consider how your product team envisions "mainstream" users and use cases and those that do not fall into that mainstream. Eric Meyer and Sara Wachter-Boettcher, authors of *Design for Real Life*, have urged product teams to consider reframing their target users to include those people who are using their solution in the messy conditions of life, whether in extreme or everyday stress. Wachter-Boettcher, in *Technically Wrong: Sexist Apps, Biased Algorithms, and Other Threats of Toxic Tech*, sheds light on how one design team at National Public Radio improved its mobile app news coverage in recognition of stress cases such as English language learners checking critical news alerts. By envisioning this and other stress-case scenarios, the team made a set of design choices that made the app easier to use in a wider variety of use cases. Thus, the team avoided relegating either specific users or use cases as "edge cases" that need not be addressed by the solution right away or at all.

Another way to use personas to identify how you may be under-serving a population is to consider minority (broadly defined) personas' *specific* interactions with your product.

Airbnb, the home-sharing platform, has updated its photo-sharing protocol to allow hosts to require guests to share photos of themselves only *after* the booking is complete to reduce the potential for racial discrimination that guests of color face prior to the booking's confirmation. The company has recognized that some guests—particularly Black males—did not want to be required to share their photos early in the process because of their experience with hosts who discriminate based on skin color. Airbnb's decision to adjust the technology to aid users in complying with the non-discrimination policy brings into focus the value of perspective-taking based on non-majority personas.

There are two challenges to think through stress cases and minority (broadly defined) personas' specific interactions with your product. The first: The idea of intentionally broadening your lens goes against orthodoxy that teams should laser-focus on specific users and use cases to make the most effective solutions, at least initially. While most would agree that a keen understanding of specific users and use cases will help you build a better solution, the advice here is to push beyond the mainstream and/or easy problems to design a more inclusive solution at the jump, as opposed to after you have received strong feedback about the shortcomings of your product.

The other challenge to using personas to identify ethical shortcomings is how to do so without provoking the ills of stereotyping. Prevailing guidance from "intentional design" experts is to focus on personas' context for using the software, prior knowledge about it, and adjacent problems and motivations related to its use as opposed to ideating based on demographic stereotypes. Depending on how extensively your team uses personas in the first place, you might consider developing personas based on the first several of the Ethics Eight questions from Chapter 1. They ask us to consider what problem(s) we aim to solve with the product and for whom. Specifically, they urge us to look into who among users is powerful, vulnerable, or forgotten, especially when it comes to intended and unintended use of the product.

TECHNIQUE 4
Take Note of Four Failure Points of Algorithms

To identify bad precedent in your product, evaluate its core algorithms. An algorithm is a process or set of rules to be followed by a computer. This certainly includes artificial intelligence/machine learning (AI/ML) algorithms whereby the set of rules automatically improves from experience, or learns, without being explicitly programmed. Cathy O'Neil, author of *Weapons of Math Destruction*, raises four fundamental questions we should be asking ourselves when we introduce algorithmic solutions to problems. These four questions include why an algorithm is superior to the current approach, its effect on users and on non-users, as well as its impact in the long run and/or at scale. O'Neil suggests that *everyone* should be asking these questions, not just data scientists and software engineers. I concur that the whole product team should internalize these questions, given their unique familiarity with the way that technology solutions are designed to scale and their role in scaling these solutions.

O'Neil succinctly packages these four questions into standards to apply to algorithmic solutions to identify failure points. The first standard is to make sure that the algorithm that we are introducing to the situation is *better* than the human process we are replacing. This forces product teams to discuss the underlying goal of a solution, not just the positive side effects of an algorithm, such as acting faster or at a larger scale. A true-to-life, if not depressing, example: The Allen Institute for Artificial Intelligence and the University of Washington developed AI named

Grover that allows users to enter a headline, which can, in seconds, generate hundreds of paragraphs of supporting text that sound like they could have been published by respected media outlets like *The New York Times*. Applying O'Neil's first standard helps us see very quickly how replacing human writers with this AI, without clear safeguards, opens us up to an infinite amount of fake news.

The second standard, which complements the persona work, is whether the algorithm exclusively fails specific people, users or non-users alike. For example, does the algorithm leverage data that is skewed in a particular way? Does it simply not work for people with specific characteristics? O'Neil recommends applying this standard to acknowledge the legally protected classes. For example, in the United States, some of the federally protected classes include race, sex, age, national origin, citizenship, religion, physical or mental disabilities, and veteran status.

Recently, a widely used and, unfortunately, racially skewed algorithm has come to light in the healthcare sector: Studies revealed how software to guide care for nearly 70 million people systematically underestimated the needs of Black patients as compared to the needs of white patients because it predicted patients' future health costs on the basis of historical costs. "It's not because people are black; it's because of the experience of being Black," says Linda Goler Bount, president and CEO of a nonprofit called Black Women's Health Imperative. Despite the seemingly race-neutral formula, the algorithm reinforced income-based inequities around insurance coverage, job security, and transportation that allow the more affluent to consume more healthcare. O'Neil's antidote: Detect ways that algorithms may reinforce skewed data.

The third standard to apply to identify a failure point is determine whether the algorithm violates anyone's rights. O'Neil encourages considering not only U.S. constitutional rights and other legal rights, but also global human rights including those that have not yet been codified. O'Neil's example here is the common practice of large companies who use personality testing, including numerous mental health-related questions, in their hiring process. Excluding candidates based on their answers to these questions can violate their rights to a fair review of their candidacy. The impact: "These algorithms have the potential to create an underclass of people who will find themselves increasingly and inexplicably shut out from normal life," says O'Neil. We must determine what in our products may have similar consequences.

The fourth standard is to evaluate algorithms in light of long-term negative consequences beyond current users. You probably have heard of Google, but have you heard of Gaggle? Gaggle tracks content of nearly 5 million K–12 students for the purpose of preventing gun violence and suicide. What are the long-term consequences of this? As the company grows, Gaggle must grapple with the rights of minors who have given their data and the consequence of this data potentially being used against them in ways that could curtail their economic prospects or even their freedom. These are big-ticket consequences of product decisions, indeed.

Applying O'Neil's four "failure point" standards to the algorithms in your product may reveal one or more ethical low points in your product that need to be addressed both urgently and thoughtfully.

TECHNIQUE 5
Review Basics of Product Law

As the previous section begins to reveal, national and state laws and regulations may provide an ethical minimum for companies to meet. Product leaders should work with their legal counsel to identify key areas where their product may be falling short of legal expectations. The old adage says if you are your own lawyer, you have a fool for a client. It is important for product leaders to know when to engage with product counselors who—in many technology companies—are eager to work in partnership with product teams to provide an overview of the laws, regulations, and basic agreements the company has with customers and/ or end users. "Product lawyers work with product managers, designers, and engineers, to create compelling risk-managed user experiences," says Adrienne Go, associate general counsel at eBay. She also warns her legal colleagues, "don't be the dream crusher," and advises them to share in the product team's goals.

As a lawyer myself, as well as a product leader, I believe product teams need to develop a basic understanding of applicable laws, regulations, and user agreements. This allows us to be the first to identify where the team may be crossing lines that impinge on users' rights as well as the commitments our companies have made to users through our agreements.

The laws of many countries protect several basic rights of individuals. For example, in the United States, the Civil Rights Act of 1964 provides protection from discrimination for protected classes. This Act paved the way for other legislation, such as the Americans with Disabilities Act, which often has implications for accessibility of software for people with disabilities. Other national laws and regulations concern specific groups, such as children under 13 years of age.

Here, it's also important to note that some rights do *not* apply to private companies. For example, the First Amendment of the U.S. Constitution protects Americans from *government* censorship or oppression based on their speech. That said, private platforms can ban speech, included federally protected forms of speech. This option creates dissonance for us as we consider the policies of extremely large private companies like Facebook and

Twitter, both global platforms with a tremendous amount of public discourse, that operate in countries with a range of approaches toward free speech.

We should also consider users' rights that derive from industry-related regulations. In the United States, you will certainly know if you are operating in a specifically regulated sector, such as education, healthcare, or personal finance. FERPA, HIPAA, and the GLBA, respectively, will ring a bell. Holding workshops with your counsel or perusing trusted internet resources to digest some of this alphabet soup is worthwhile because changes in regulations often introduce new dynamics and opportunities in terms of product design and development.

Finally, product professionals should consider the basics of customer contracts, including the terms of use (TOU) and the disclosures we should be making to our users. Here we have an opportunity to consider how to make TOUs as clear as possible and improve their accuracy and transparency. We must give users a legitimate chance to read and understand the agreements they are making when they click consent buttons. These agreements are notoriously difficult to read and understand. This, in part, contributes to the fact that hardly anyone reads them.

Academic researchers made up a social networking site called Name Drop and asked study participants to sign up to use it, after agreeing to the site's terms and services. In this experiment, the terms stated that users' personal information would be shared with the National Security Agency (NSA) and that the company that owns the site will take users' firstborn children as payment for use. Ninety-eight percent of the study volunteers agreed to give up their children, while only one individual in the 500-person study objected to the NSA policy.

Here, I urge us to champion the change we wish to see. As product leaders, we ought to review the agreements our companies have with our customers, such as the TOU, the privacy policy, and other possible terms and addenda. One product professional, whose company has a fairly industry-standard TOU shared a comment from an end user about it, surprised that it was even read by a user in the first place: "You are not responsible for receiving my communications or honoring my settings? You have an eternal license to use my info for literally any future use, depending on how you change, which you are also not responsible for alerting me to? No thx." The opportunity is upon us to explain this better and ideate ways to create more transparency for users. After all, isn't that our job?

TECHNIQUE 6
Look Around: Research Better and Best Practices

Exploring the norms around you can help you improve key areas where you fall short from an ethics standpoint. Note, though, that while norms can indicate areas for improvement, they should not be your sole aspiration. The PCOE remains the north star. That said, you can look to the set of technologies you and your customers use or could use (i.e., your competitors) to understand where you may be falling short.

> » What does your competitors' product marketing entail?
> » What kinds of users do your competitors serve that you are overlooking?
> » What unintended consequences does their approach have? Does your approach have the same unintended consequences?
> » How do your competitors appear to be keeping up or not keeping up with evolving regulations?
> » What notions of privacy do these technologies encompass?

» In what ways can you create better agreements with your customers about how you will go about solving their problems?

Sound familiar? They come from the Ethics Eight. These are extremely important questions to ask when creating durable value for your customers, given the alternative solutions they can be choosing.

If you are ahead of the pack, consider investing even further in your "above average" approach to use these victories as differentiators. Also, many product teams, on their scale journey, consider partnership opportunities with these same third parties. Gaining familiarity with competitors' approaches and their PCOEs can help you see when you should run toward a symbiotic opportunity or flee an ethical landmine.

TECHNIQUE 7
Don't Waste a Crisis: Yours, Someone Else's, or a Pending One

I originally wrote this section prior to the global coronavirus pandemic, defining a crisis as an event more specific to a product in question, like a security breach. The point that I was making was that scenario-planning and thinking through the anatomy of a product crisis is a good blueprint for plotting out what to do if your team had an unexpected, usually unwelcome, opportunity to improve your software for consumers.

Then, in March 2020, the worldwide pandemic gave many of us just this chance to consider how to evolve our products and services to support our customers during this uncertain time. In April and May, my colleagues and I stepped through the process below, as did most of my peers at other companies:

» Develop a response plan, including a chain of command about the response.

» Determine a data management system for questions/feedback/complaints.
» Plan a method to communicate with customers and the community (via social media if appropriate) to keep the public informed about your response.

Then, in June, in the United States and beyond, the public has acknowledged an additional longstanding crisis of racial injustice, horrifically displayed by the murder of George Floyd by police. Those of us working on products in 2020 during both crises, have needed to mobilize, or I should say "virtualize," in some way to support colleagues and customers. If you were part of a large, consumer-facing company, the court of public opinion evaluated your team's actions; if you were below the public radar, at a minimum, every person at your company began to evaluate the value you deliver through your software and how to amplify it during a time of great uncertainty. And across this time, your team took a series of actions or inactions that are worth reviewing from an ethical standpoint to help you sharpen, now, what you need to address.

Here are three questions that you can ask in the aftermath of a crisis:

1. What was your product team's response?
   - What product decisions did you make?
   - Can you apply the Ethics Eight to those decisions?
   - What was positive about your response?
   - What gaps or opportunities remain?

2. Did you have a PCOE in place that helped you clarify your response? If not, how you would create or evolve one to serve your users better?

3. What, if any, low points or bad precedents need to be addressed now based on the new realities of your users' lives?

TAKEAWAYS FROM THIS CHAPTER

- **Technique 3 of 20:** Use personas intentionally. Consider how your product is used by people and how to address use cases that fall outside of "mainstream" or "happy path" scenarios.
- **Technique 4 of 20:** Consider scale when you evaluate algorithmic solutions to user problems and apply O'Neil's four standards to avoid "mass destruction."
- **Technique 5 of 20:** It's worth developing a training workshop on the laws that govern your enterprise and the basic agreements between your company and your customers.
- **Technique 6 of 20:** Look at the practices of companies within and outside of your industry to identify where your company may be falling short.
- **Technique 7 of 20:** One of the most valuable future scenarios to play out is ethical crisis management, to equip your team to avoid a crisis in the first place or to respond effectively when one arises.

CHAPTER 4: BAKE ETHICS INTO YOUR PRODUCT DEVELOPMENT PROCESS

Working through the previous chapter, you must have found a few low points to address and are preparing to make a convincing case to your colleagues to do so. Maybe you have gone so far as to put these items on your product roadmap. You most likely have a product development process in place that involves ceremonies related to software development stages: discovery of the problem-to-be-solved; designing, building, and testing possible solutions; and releasing the solution.

Rather than establishing a separate process—an "ethics process"—the more surefire approach would be to incorporate PCOE standards into your current process so that you can release the most ethical product you can straight out of the gate. In personal development, this is known as habit stacking. People who meditate just after brushing their teeth are more likely to keep up with meditation. Ethical decision-making habits get entrenched with activities already in practice, like QA testing code before releasing it. You can reduce the risk of releasing low-ethics features by evolving the methods of your existing product development process. After all, if the widespread reaction is "you should've known better than to launch with this," your process is most likely to blame. That said, the release of a feature is only the beginning: The way users use and perceive the feature *in the real world over time* warrants intense cycles of listening and learning so that you can improve the feature. Thus, the product development process—with ethical decision-making incorporated into each step, including monitoring post-launch—will help your product meet a higher ethical bar.

DISCOVERY PHASE
Define the Problem-to-be Solved... Responsibly

During the discovery phase, do this one thing: Set "responsible" metrics for product and feature success. An emerging best practice in the field of product development is for product teams to frame the goal of a feature's development into a measurable result, that teams can then decompose into changes in human behavior that have a high likelihood of leading to the result. For example, a team that wants to increase online purchases might observe that people who read product reviews on their site tend to purchase products at a higher rate. Thus, the team can design "experiments" around those actual observable changes in behavior and see how those behaviors impact the business results. In this example, they might design a series of experiments to get users to read more reviews.

Once you can identify the business result and the change in behavior that is likely to drive it, you can then ask whether *each* meets a high ethical standard. To identify the ethical bar for the business result, the technique I like to use is to add the word *responsible* to the key performance indicator in question, such as *responsible* "increase in x" or *responsible* "reduction of y." So, in the example just mentioned, the team might want to see a responsible "increase in online sales"; if the team is considering concepts to increase readership of legitimate reviews, they might also think through how to discourage fake reviews or other gaming of reviews that may be considered unethical. They might ask themselves about unintended use, the fourth area of the Ethics Eight from Chapter 1.

Setting a "responsible" metric and identifying ways to reach it, also responsibly, is tough, nuanced, and will inevitably be ongoing. YouTube has been trying to establish a responsible metric: "quality watch time" with the goal of encouraging user behavior that will benefit advertisers, yet reduce addictive viewing or viewing that could be deemed as socially corrosive because of the nature of the content. To get at the quality part of the watch-time metric, the team associates watch time with other metrics concerning viewer surveys, the sharing of clips, and likes versus dislikes. Note that in using these metrics, the YouTube team is wrestling with the adequacy of human versus machine judgment and is still working through assumptions. For example, the assumption that extremist content, like videos promoting white supremacy, will be received negatively by their target audience is a flawed assumption according to Becca Lewis, a Stanford University researcher who studies YouTube. Unfortunately, these videos are extremely popular, receiving lots of likes from viewers.

That said, the setting of the watch-time metrics and encouraging behavior that would drive the metrics, including the remuneration of video creators, has a huge impact on advertisement-based revenue growth as well as the spread of content. After YouTube stripped ads from videos it deemed questionable, some channels were said to have lost millions of dollars in ad sales. Whether this is good or bad is complicated. The takeaway is to use the discovery process in your product development process to set ethical targets on both the desired high-level result and the behavior changes that would lead to that result; again, you would do this, not because the process is easy but because the nuance matters.

Almost all product features used in excess or in a specific way can be harmful. Screen time is one example; expressing oneself publicly is another; relying on algorithms to make decisions is yet another. Sometimes we figure out that the fundamental business model conflicts with some of our values as a society and thus must be addressed at the business model level; even with that, guardrails on features themselves must be set *responsibly*. Your team can go about this much more easily with a PCOE in hand and principle champions advocating for alignment between the desired outcome of your features and the PCOE.

DESIGN PHASE
Expand High Ethics Alternatives
Once your product team has discovered the problem to be addressed and set responsible success metrics as suggested by the last technique, the next step is to develop several

alternatives to address it. Design experts urge us not only to generate technology-based alternatives to solve the business problem, but also to brainstorm non-technical solutions such as new services, policies, business models, and the like. These next three techniques help you generate ethical alternatives, evaluate those alternatives from multiple angles, and select a winning solution.

Generate Ethical Alternatives With Crazy Eights, Ethics Style

To generate ideas, use any innovative design practices that work for your team. Crazy Eights, made popular in *Sprint* by Jake Knapp, is one technique that I've found effective in refining alternatives to address ethical issues. Using their strongest ideas as a starting point, each person rapidly sketches eight variations in eight minutes. This forces designers to tweak and expand on one or two solid ideas to improve their ethical ramifications. All you need: a sheet of letter-size paper to fold into eight panels and the prompt, "What would be another good way to do this?" The technique works well for visualization as well as copywriting.

Evaluate Alternatives With the Tarot Cards of Tech

A Seattle-based design firm, the Artefact Group, created a free printable quirky deck of question cards to help teams ask ethics-related questions about design alternatives. The Tarot Cards of Tech help designers foresee unintended consequences and develop solutions to create a positive impact. The Big Bad Wolf card asks, "What could a bad actor do with your product?" The Service Dog card asks, "If your product was entirely dedicated to empowering the lives of an under-served population, what kind of impact could you make?" Rather than "Move fast and break things," the Artefact Group recommends that we "slow down and ask the right questions."

Select a Winning Solution by Articulating and Testing Your Hypotheses

By asking questions upfront, develop several ethics-aware alternatives that can compete to win out from an ethics standpoint. For each alternative, the team can articulate, "we believe" testable hypothesis statements: "We believe that [business outcome] will be achieved if [user] attains [benefit] with [solution]." The "we believe" language sets a healthy tone of conviction about potential ethical choice points. For example, a common pair of alternatives pits a prescriptive default against a configurable set of choices in user settings. Facing these alternatives, Firefox completed several usability tests to develop a solution to block third-party trackers that collect user data by default. One of the tests that Firefox ran was a study of how much of the total time required to load a website is spent loading third-party trackers. With that evidence, Firefox made the choice it deemed best for users: The team set the blocking as the default versus requiring users to adjust their own settings.

>Here's an example of a testable hypothesis statement:

>*We believe that the volume of search usage and associated ad revenue, based on better user experience—faster load time—will outweigh user data revenue if our users can arrive at their content more quickly with a default block on third-party tracking.*

BUILD PHASE
Define and Document Ethics Requirements

The agile software development process articulates how to write user requirements through stories. These stories have a structure, complete with the "so what," to help engineers meet the requirement. Here, I advocate applying a couple of well-known formats to document your product's ethics requirements across the build process: Amazon's internal press release and six-page memo formats. These two formats can elegantly capture ethics requirements across the build process.

Nextdoor uses the memo process to support ethical decision-making. Nextdoor wants to build a product that fosters community and belonging and avoid ethical pitfalls like biased profiling, public shaming, threats, and excessive profanity. Tatyana Mamut, chief product officer at Nextdoor—whose corporate mission it is to build stronger local communities—describes this press release and memo exercise as an optimal way to "put the customer at the center when working on product definition." Nextdoor has invested in their Kindness Reminder feature that presents users—who have drafted questionable content in their post—with an editing opportunity before posting. Nextdoor's internal memos have made their way into a fully published blog post about the creation of this feature. See Reading List under Technique 13.

Memos
Amazon Internal Press Release and Six-Page Memo Formats
Here's how to use Amazon's memo formats to document your product's ethics requirements. Ironically, you begin the process by writing up a fake press release. Amazon's internal press release structure originates in the land of make-believe. It introduces the product and target user and succinctly describes the product and the benefit, as a solution to a problem. Next, it includes a quote from a company spokesperson to bring the benefit to life, such as, "Amazon customers want same-day deliveries. We created Prime and PrimeNow to provide our customers with deliveries in as little as two hours," states Amazon founder, Jeff Bezos. The press release

closes with a call-to-action on getting started and a quote from a customer describing how *they* experienced the solution's benefit. The aspirational press-release paints a picture of value that your product can deliver to the customer.

Pairing the aspirational press-release with the six-page internal memo format helps the team make decisions along the development process that improve the ethical impact of the product. The Amazon memo format follows a slightly less formulaic template than the press-release—though reading the memo in silence at the start of meetings is famously required. The memo always covers three critical subjects: first, the point or objective of the project or question at hand, that is, the "so what" of why the company should care about the topic; second, how teams have attempted to handle this issue in the past and how the presenter's attempt differs from prior; and, third, counterarguments to the presenter's arguments.

The pair of formats, as is, lend themselves nicely to reasoned decision-making across the build cycle, which is why they withstand the test of time at Amazon and at other companies. As a way to express ethics requirements, the formats provide opportunities to express nuance about the ethical underpinnings of the problem and aspects of the proposed solution, as long as the team remembers to consider the breadth of the problem to be solved and defines the customer and their user context holistically, perhaps thinking not only of a human-centered discussion but also of a humanity-centered one. (Perhaps the Prime team can write a memo on what Amazon can do to help users minimize their carbon footprint!).

My own experience supports the use of the internal press release and the six-page memo methodology as a useful way to work with cross-functional teams on complex software during the build phase. By providing a true north—in the form of the press release—and by laying out decision-making via the memos as the project evolves, these documents are particularly powerful for raising the ethical bar and associated decision-making. Specifically, they allow your whole team, writers and readers alike, to benefit from what is known in ethics as the Sunlight Test: Would I do the same thing if I knew my actions would end up on the front page of the newspaper tomorrow?

It's not about whether these internal press releases and memos will be published, though companies like Nextdoor are increasingly publishing their product development journey in blog posts; rather, it's about adopting, through the build process, a mindset of full transparency about the goals and decisions the team is making along the way.

TEST PHASE
Build Ethics Into Internal and External Testing

Prior to making your software generally available, your team likely performs a variety of tests internally and with a limited group of external end users. This testing, which has a set of ethics of its own, is critically important as a preventative tool for ethical crises. As far as prevention goes, makers and users of products—all of us—understand that many problems become visible or emerge only after shipping. However, the value of internal testing, from an ethics perspective, helps to stave off many scenarios that scream of "you should have anticipated this!"

Internal Quality Assurance

As with other parts of the product development process, the key to *ethical* quality assurance testing is to incorporate it into an existing practice. Ethical quality assurance becomes a worthwhile habit coupled with others, like debugging code before releasing it into production. Here are two strategies to enable internal ethical quality assurance tactics to take hold.

The first: Just prior to sprint team demos, which many agile teams do every couple of weeks, ask the team to look at the PCOE and the Ethics Eight to prime them to capture concerns with what they see. Discuss whether stress cases or forgotten personas have emerged and document those, along with other salient gaps, for the team to address. Agree on what to address and commit to including these new scenarios in later tests.

The second: If your team is not already in the practice of doing so, consider incorporating an Inspect & Adapt (I&A) event, a ceremony from the scaled agile framework, software development protocol increasingly being adopted by larger software companies. Larger software development teams pursue I&A as a regular event during which the sprint teams demonstrate what they've built across a period, to the entire software development organization, including stakeholders, before releasing those items into production. In addition to the broader demonstration, the I&A event also entails reviewing quantitative and qualitative data collected, a retrospective, and a problem-solving workshop, all designed to help the team make necessary adjustments.

This I&A event lends itself well to internal quality assurance from an ethics standpoint. Like with the sprint team demos, everyone participating in this event, often *all* of the key stakeholders, can review the PCOE and the Ethics Eight, perhaps assigning participants specific principles and question sets to evaluate in advance. Software teams that run these I&A events successfully emphasize the importance of demonstrating the feature in a way that is as true-to-life as possible, both because product-centered versus human-centered demos often bore people and the odds of identifying new issues that the team has overlooked improves when the team can imagine the feature in use. Where possible, leverage personas and vivid storylines to help the team evaluate where the solution may fall short from an ethics standpoint and how it can be strengthened.

As a product leader, do what you can to recognize aspects of group thinking and blind spots in your organizational culture, which can lead to poor design and move toward an increasingly inclusive team. Here, again, it's worth mentioning the dire need for diversity, equity, and inclusion within the software development and stakeholder team. See Reading List, as this is a topic of extensive discussion in pockets, with no easy or short-term solutions.

For nearly all B2B companies, the above methods of inspecting the product internally will be the logical stopping point; however, many companies that create software for individual consumers set up a protocol to use the product internally to test actual usage. This concept is called "dogfooding" or "drinking your own champagne" and, in the right conditions, allows internal validation on several different levels before the software is rolled out to early access customers or the general user base.

External Early-Release Testing

After internal review, most technology companies conduct end-user early-release (alpha and beta) testing as they release updates to their software. Target users validate the user experience of the product over a defined period of time, providing feedback on the usability of the design and value of the functionality. Here is an opportunity to introduce an ethics lens as you construct alpha and beta tests with real people, in real environments, using the product. Swing toward as broad a cross section of real users as possible.

The steps to set up early-release testing generally include planning, recruiting, rolling out the test package, collecting and evaluating feedback, and closing out the test. When defining the goals of the beta, part of the scope could be evaluation of specific ethical hotspots. How do you know what to test for at this stage? If you completed an internal dogfooding or review, you may have surfaced ethical tensions based on the Ethics Eight and/or from evaluating how well the solution reinforces your PCOE.

Hypothetically, let's say we work on a personal finance app and that we have established a PCOE with the principle: "Explain to consumers the reasoning behind recommendations." Let's say that we're now introducing AI-driven nudge features. In the beta, we can A/B test which "nudge" copy scores better from an "explain-ability" standpoint *and* produces the desired behavior in the application. With these results in hand, we can interview beta participants about how well they understood the app's recommendations, knowing that transparency of recommendations is one of our PCOE principles.

Two important considerations arise at the stage of constructing the early-release test: the ethics of the testing goals and—once these goals are established—a process of gathering informed consent from participants. Informed consent is explicit permission from participants to be involved in research, once they understand the goals of the project and the research methods.

The notorious experimental study that Facebook conducted in 2012 might pop into your mind for its lack of informed consent. The company expressly set out to study "emotional contagion through social networks." Facebook experimented on nearly 700,000 of its users to determine the behavioral impact of adjusting its News Feed feature, such as the effect of filtering

CHAPTER 4: BAKE ETHICS INTO YOUR PRODUCT DEVELOPMENT PROCESS

out "negative" news versus "positive" news. The goal was to measure the impact of Facebook's filters on user behavior, such as setting statuses or responding to posts (Likes). Instead of collecting informed consent, Facebook relied on its broad data-use policy that allows for research and service improvement. There was public outcry about the approach Facebook took. Given that Facebook's data-use policy is standard language for most technology companies, the tip here is to be very cautious about the protocol of working with human subjects, especially with anything as sensitive as psychological manipulation based on filtering news.

While this example from Facebook appears extreme on the surface, you may be asking yourself: Is every update to the software a kind of experiment that requires informed consent? The answer is no. Most software updates, such as a newly designed navigation bar or a feature that makes it easier to receive customer service, will fall nicely into your software's data-use policy. That said, it's a good idea—for all your updates—to write an internal press release (à la the Amazon format) that can then easily be turned into an engaging release note. In it, you will identify the anticipated benefits and potential risks of the update. If the risks are minimal, you can rest assured that you can respond to feedback in due course about the update. If the risks are material, more testing may be required. Gather informed consent from participants, by clearly stating the research goals, the product decisions the research would support, and the exact risks involved. If characterizing the risks as minimal versus material is difficult, err on the side of conducting additional testing with informed consent.

When it comes to recruiting participants, your ability to surface ethics issues to get a read on the decisions already made improves with a diverse base of those who will likely use your product. One senior product leader encourages her team to push hard to recruit a very diverse user base for testing, even more diverse than the current user base to invite use from a broader cross section of potential, yet real, people. Using a sports metaphor and a cliché, this is the idea of "skating to where the puck is going" versus where it has been.

In rolling out the test package, it would be important to create as much of a real-world context as possible for your testers. For example, you might consider sending them an up-to-date internal press release, including the call-to-action. Consider also introducing the actual user manuals, guides, and known issues. With all of this, clarify for your testers the best procedures to log ethical concerns. Finally, per best practices in early-release test design, consider—in advance—how you will evaluate the input. Specifically consider what you will do with the ethics-related feedback you collect. For example, will you consider expanding the "known issues" area in your release notes when you make the technology generally available? If your users vote with their clicks or comments in a certain way, would you consider adjusting your product to incorporate the input? When you close the test, will you keep in touch with participants who gave you valuable ethics-related feedback?

POST-LAUNCH
Help Your Team Maintain Focus on Ethics

To come full circle to the idea at the beginning of the chapter, best practice in product management encourages teams to maintain the discipline of revisiting the feature after shipping it to ask whether people are using the feature at all, using it as we—as makers—expect and getting the value that they—as users—expect. This discipline is key in practice, but hinges on the clarity of knowing what the team expects to see in terms of user behavior and thinking through how to course-correct if user behavior veers off-course.

Adopt the Discipline of Monitoring User Behavior and Its Relationship With Results

Product leaders must understand that releasing a product is just the beginning and not the end of the process. Many ethical issues come to light as the product is used and evaluated. These shortcomings are often collected in an enhancement backlog while product teams have mostly moved on to the "next thing." Regardless of what companies say, product leaders contend with a harsh reality of resource constraints.

This next technique, very simple at first glance, begins to address the complicated struggle to find space in your roadmap to improve existing features, including from an ethical standpoint. As product managers increasingly share their roadmaps internally and externally with their customers, they are doing so in the form of problems they are exploring "Now," "Next," and "Later." A few years ago, I came across this flexible problem versus feature-oriented roadmap layout via Prodpad, makers of roadmap software for product managers. More recently, some companies that use this format have added one additional time frame to the roadmap to precede "Now": a column for "Last." This column covers what was released in the prior time frame. Maintaining this column on your roadmap serves as a visual reminder to evaluate—with regularity—the impact of what was last released, including its ethical impact. This transparency encourages everyone who prioritizes the roadmap to at least consider whether new endeavors should be prioritized over improvements to recently released items.

LAST	NOW	NEXT	LATER
Improve workflow » Feature 1 & hypothesized benefit	**Improve workflow** » Feature 2 & hypothesized benefit	**Improve accessibility** » Mobile feature 6 & hypothesized benefit	**Improve workflow** » Feature 1 & hypothesized benefit
Provide automation » Feature 6 & hypothesized benefit	**Improve data privacy** » Feature 3 & hypothesized benefit	**Improve automation** » Feature 6 & hypothesized benefit	**Improve support** » Feature 4 & hypothesized benefit

The ideas for ethical improvements can come from your analysis of whether, how, and to what end the feature is being used. They can also come from new answers to the Ethics Eight, which you can revisit on the same cadence as you update the roadmap, so that you're reviewing ethical impact in a regular rhythm.

The ideas can also come from taking an approach grounded in behavioral science, a field that looks at the gap between what people want to do and what they *actually* do. In his book, *Start at the End*, Matt Wallaert introduces the Intervention Design Process, a process that can be applied to newly released or existing features, or "interventions." The approach helps product teams ensure that the interventions contribute to desired behavior.

The process is best explained by Wallaert's work on Microsoft's Bing search engine, post-release. After some quantitative and qualitative research of users' search behavior, Wallaert articulated a behavioral statement that described the endpoint the team desired: "When students have a curiosity question, and they are in school and near a computer with internet connectivity, they'll use Bing to answer it, as measured by queries per student." The team then generated a list of promoting pressures (tailwinds) and inhibiting pressures (headwinds) for the desired behavior.

User research revealed that teachers faced four inhibiting pressures that impacted their behavior, which led to lower-than-expected Bing searches by students. Teachers worried about online safety, advertising, privacy, and distraction from the curriculum. After understanding these four inhibiting pressures and designing ethical interventions specifically to remove these pressures, Wallaert's team convened people across Microsoft and from an external policy think tank to assess the ethics and surface blind spots. After piloting simple versions of the interventions and seeing results, Microsoft scaled those via "Bing in the Classroom," increasing search in schools by 40 percent and forcing its competitor, Google, to turn off ads in the classroom.

At a minimum, as product leaders articulate what to work on next, understanding—with an ethical lens—the promoting and inhibiting pressures for the desired behavior within existing features enables teams to raise the ethics of their solution.

Communicate With Your Users About Product Ethics

With today's technology, product teams can have an almost live dialogue with their end users. You can imagine conversations in which designers ask select users what leads them to use the product or not and what concerns they have. Use your product advisory council to collect input about the ethical dimensions of your product. Ask members of these groups to pressure-test, as transparently as possible, the alternative options your team faces. For example, you can cover "ethical use of data" as a standing topic with your product advisory council, bringing to them new and nuanced scenarios about the possible ways you can serve your target market.

To go a step further beyond members of a council, I encourage you to take an even more proactive in-app approach to develop an ethics feedback loop within the product. Many applications now provide "contextual help," also known as context-sensitive help, in the form of tool tips, walk-throughs, and embedded prompts to make it more convenient for end users to stay within the app while resolving their questions about its use. You may remember Clippy, the animated paper clip in Microsoft? Technology has come a long way since. Contextual help is now considered an essential part of good online service because it does not disrupt the user's workflow or waste their time by forcing them to search through lengthy manuals. More recently, many applications have also taken to eliciting input from users in context. Putting these ideas together, product teams can scale some forms of ethical dialogue by "conversing" with users in the app. You can introduce lightweight surveys about user preferences, while targeting information to users through tooltips, release notes, and other areas of the product, such as a "privacy center."

There are several in-app survey best practices that are worth reviewing. The best practices cover how to clarify the goal of the survey and the target sample—which should be developed with diversity in mind and/or randomized as appropriate. Understandably, the users of the software itself are a narrow sample; people who don't use the software can provide valuable insight as to why. Thus, these same questions can be asked, perhaps through a network created by your product advisory council, to people who do not use the application.

Responses can be compared across different populations of users (and non-users) to reveal useful perspectives of who is (and who is not) well served by the feature or app as a whole and what they do (and do not) appreciate about the service:

1. What concerns you about the app? *(text field)*

2. Which feature of the app is most/least important to you? *(multiple choice)*

3. Which features didn't work as expected? *(text field)*

4. What keeps you from using this feature? *(text field)*

5. What language in the app has confused/annoyed/offended you? *(text field)*

6. How clear do you find our terms of use *(scale of 1-5)*

Whether due to pressure or on their own accord, many companies now strive to communicate with their end users more clearly and regularly about features and related policies.

TAKEAWAYS FROM THIS CHAPTER

- **Technique 8 of 20:** To discover ethical solutions, you must raise ethical standards in both the desired results and the changes in behavior that would lead to them.
- **Technique 9 of 20:** In the design phase, generate a large volume of high-ethics alternatives, using the Crazy Eights Method.
- **Technique 10 of 20:** Once you have alternatives, use the Tarot Cards of Tech to ask questions of your alternatives.

- » **Technique 11 of 20:** In finalizing alternatives to evaluate, develop hypothesis statements to design experiments to predict your odds of producing desired ethical outcomes.
- » **Technique 12 of 20:** Start your build phase *after* you have clarified the big picture through an internal press release.
- » **Technique 13 of 20:** In the build phase, formally document ethics requirements and decision-making through structured memos.
- » **Technique 14 of 20:** In the test phase, incorporate ethics into internal quality assurance.
- » **Technique 15 of 20:** Incorporate ethics into alpha and beta testing.
- » **Technique 16 of 20:** Post-launch, see released features as the beginning of the work as opposed to the end. Apply a behavioral science-based approach to clarifying "promoting" and "inhibiting" pressures. This enables product teams to focus on driving outcomes ethically.
- » **Technique 17 of 20:** Post-launch, engage in an ongoing in-app dialogue with your end users. This is a great way to stay committed to improving the ethical impact of your solution.

CHAPTER 5: STAY PERSONALLY COMMITTED TO ETHICAL PRODUCT DEVELOPMENT

While the previous chapters were about product professionals working with *teams* to establish the PCOE and adhere to processes to improve the ethical trajectory of their product choices, this chapter is about inspiring *individuals* to stay personally committed to their ethical codes in the face of competing pressures. Here are three techniques that inspire me that I want to share with you.

ESTABLISH YOUR CAREER CODE OF ETHICS

Take an hour to write down your personal professional code of ethics if you have not had occasion to do so thus far in your working life. It will serve as your compass in the face of diverging pressures. Dexter, my favorite fictional serial killer, follows The Code of Harry, which contains a simple guideline: Kill people *only* after finding conclusive evidence that they are guilty of murder. This code really helped Dexter to raise the ethical bar of his pursuits; a simple code like this can help you, too.

KEY QUESTIONS FOR YOUR CAREER CODE OF ETHICS

The process starts with questions like those in the Ethics Eight about your purpose, supplemented with questions about how you aim to operate. With a little time to reflect, product leaders find the first three basic questions both fun and straightforward to answer. Their answers often clarify why they find themselves in product development in the first place.

1. Who do I most want to help?

2. What problem do I most want to solve?

3. What solution do I most want to provide?

To write your Personal Professional Code of Ethics, you can supplement these questions with a few more:

4. What personal values underlie my work?
   In other words, why do I care about this work?

5. How will I improve my ability to serve?

6. What concerns me about the work that I do?

7. What can I do to address those concerns?

Write out the answers, in pencil. A few days later take some time to reflect on what you have written. In the same way that the PCOE reflects company values, your personal professional code of ethics reflects your personal values. As a product leader, you are in a unique position to incorporate these into your work. Reid Hoffman, founder of LinkedIn, has a theory that every great founder has a second purpose: to get something good done in the world outside their core business. Just a few examples are to equalize opportunities, connect people, spark creativity, use data to make decisions. Many product leaders, either consciously or subconsciously, toil in service of that second purpose.

If that second purpose is not yet evident to you as the basis for developing your personal code, you might also look to certain role-based codes to design your personal code. Unlike the medical and legal professions, the product development field does not have a universal code of ethics. Software engineers sometimes look to the eight principles from the IEEE Computer Society. Two principles among them:

1. To engineer software that is consistent with the public interest

2. To ensure that products they develop meet the highest professional standards possible

These are a little broad in my opinion, but they may inspire you to refine your own with regard to aspects of public interest or the definition of professional standards.

Radhika Dutt, co-founder of Radical Product Thinking, and someone who considers each product as a product leader's mechanism for creating change in the world, advocates for a Hippocratic oath for product leaders. She encourages them—like medical doctors—to take full responsibility for the solutions they prescribe. To this end, Dutt suggests a principle that is very much worth more of us championing: "Separate your product vision from your business goals: Always two there are." Dutt recounts, "I often see vision statements such as 'to change how people communicate and become a billion-dollar company in the process.'" She then asks us to imagine our doctor's vision statement: "To cure patients' ailments and build a practice of over $1M a year." She suggests that vision statements like these make it easy to lose sight of the change you wanted to create in the first place.

In response to the business-minded among us who ask, "where should the financial goal go?" I would say it goes wherever your enterprise logs its financial goals, not in the vision statement. Dutt's principle is to prioritize distinctive activities that help you make progress toward a vision. And there's ample evidence that her principle pans out.

In 1994, Jim Collins and Jerry Porras, in *Good to Great*, showcased how a set of companies guided by purpose (beyond generating profit) returned six times more value to shareholders than their explicitly profit-driven rivals. Since then, many studies have replicated this finding for companies and for individuals. Personally, this gives me confidence to double-down on establishing and refining my own principles and purpose because this commitment to purpose proves to be economically beneficial for companies over the long run.

CHAPTER 5: STAY PERSONALLY COMMITTED TO ETHICAL PRODUCT DEVELOPMENT

SAMPLE PERSONAL PROFESSIONAL CODE OF ETHICS

To produce [ethical products] for [my users], I will

- » Separate vision from financial goals: "Always two there are"; thus, I will choose to invest consistently in making progress toward vision.
- » In working with data, take the perspective of each user, as a real person in considering fairness, validity, anonymity, privacy, ownership, and volition. Also, take the perspective of "the system," to clarify how *my* actions ossify current state, amplify historical bias, or serve to produce positive change.
- » Keep a journal of choices that I anticipate will lead to more positive impact.
- » Commit to growth in ethical product development by
  - Taking on new challenges; practicing having a "possibilist" mindset as I develop new skills *and* perspectives
  - Observing and learning from the work of [role models in my field]
  - Collaborating with colleagues who challenge me
  - Celebrating evolution in myself and others

BUILD EMPATHY THROUGH ETHNOGRAPHIC AND DIARY RESEARCH

While ethnographic and diary research techniques can fit into areas of the process I outlined in prior chapters, such as during the discovery, design, or testing phases or as part of ongoing communication with your end users, post-launch, I'm covering the techniques here because of how valuable they prove to be to product professionals themselves, in inspiring them to produce ethical products. Most people who use these techniques transform their approach. They come away with greater empathy for users, as well as for themselves as people working on the users' behalf; they understand the problems they are solving more deeply; they can envision—with more clarity—aspects of a solution they aspire to deliver. My peers routinely say that ethnographic and diary research gives them direct, real-life insight into the pain points of users' lives. And that this helps them build better products.

Regardless of your role in the product development process, I encourage you to work with your user experience colleagues to participate in these two forms of research. Both ethnographic and diary research techniques themselves have ethical considerations ranging from informed consent to confidentiality and privacy. Assuming you work through these protocols, these two research techniques can give you uniquely strong backing for ethical decision-making and refresh your desire and ability to serve your users, addressing their problems in a fuller context.

Ethnographic Research: In ethnography, there are five potential "observer" roles that you may consider taking to understand what your users experience. They range from "off-site" observer (e.g., the ethnographer merely reads posts in an online community) all the way to a complete participant (e.g., the ethnographer conducts financial transactions using cryptocurrency). The more involved you get, the greater your opportunity to experience firsthand what users experience. Each of the five observer roles offers a unique vantage point in terms of psychological or emotional distance from the process; thus, you can gain different layers of insight as you immerse yourself with your users. Whichever observer role you choose—or that the logistics of the scenario dictate—err on the side of being overt versus covert in your participation, so as not to deceive the users whom you are trying to understand better.

Diary Research: Diary research calls for participants to log their thoughts and experiences about a product, process, or activity in their real-world environment across a time frame of a few days up to a few months. It gets into the nitty-gritty of what motivates users to take certain actions, why they engage in certain behaviors, and their attitudes. Today, researchers often conduct these studies online, asking participants to use a smart phone to log their input, depending on what is being studied. Diary research calls for users to make regular entries, such as free-form texts, videos, or audio recordings.

Global online learning platform Udemy used the diary study methodology to understand how students use its platform with both desktop and mobile devices. "Basically, each time a student used Udemy, we asked them to use the camera on their mobile phone to show us where they were and what they were doing, including their environment and the context around that specific moment," researcher Michelle Fiesta explains. Janel Faucher, Udemy's senior UX researcher describes how this study reflects how Udemy "operates from a very learning-driven, empathetic mindset. Udemy employees want to hear what our users have to say."

LEAD WITH HUMILITY AND FIERCE RESOLVE WHILE LEARNING FROM OTHER PEOPLE

Jim Collins, co-author of Good to Great defines a Level 5 leader as the kind of leader that seeks to build something larger and more lasting than themselves. He opines that the four other levels (contributing as an individual, a team member, a manager, and an effective leader) are coachable. In contrast, Level 5 requires leaders to be predisposed to see more value in what they build, create, and contribute than in personal gains from their work.

> *"Level 5 leaders display a powerful mixture of personal humility and indomitable will. They're incredibly ambitious, but their ambition is first and foremost for the cause, for the organization and its purpose, not themselves. While Level 5 leaders can come in many personality packages, they are often self-effacing, quiet, researched, and even shy. Every good-to-great transition in our research began with a Level 5 leader who motivated the enterprise more with inspired standards than inspiring personality."*
> —Jim Collins

I believe that most product leaders have this seed in them. But the question is how do you become a Level 5 leader? Collins—possibly sparking frustration—does not think it's possible to get there through deliberate steps. His main recommendation is to pursue reflective character development through personal enrichment activities, a mentor, a great teacher, loving relationships, a Level 5 boss, or a significant life experience.

For me, the key aspects to moving toward Level 5 in ethical product leadership include cultivating humility and fierce resolve, while learning from other people. In my experience, it has been useful to seek out the wisdom of people outside my everyday world. For example, it has been useful to follow the efforts of people like Tristan Harris, former design ethicist at Google, who was the original champion of the effort to encourage tech companies to focus on helping users spend their time well. Or Vijaya Gadde, Twitter's head of legal, public policy, trust and safety, who helps Twitter update the platform to reduce abuse. Like Harris and Gadde, we can think about the unintended consequences of our products and rally for something better. Or people like Dong Nguyen, an independent developer of an addictive game called

Flappy Bird, that made him $50,000 per day, who—on his own accord—decided to remove the app and continue to develop games that are not addictive. He said that his conscience was relieved after he took down the game. Or more recently, after observing Eric Yuan and team's swift handling of privacy at Zoom, I felt motivated to run at some under-developed aspects of the software I work on in my day job.

Emboldened by these journeys, you can rectify actions that weigh on your conscience and take actions that make you proud. The actions you take that increase the pride you have in your work may be operational ones, in service of better serving unique users and communities. They may also require taking a stance when it comes to voting with your feet on the types of technology you personally will and will not develop. This might mean that you must decide whether to walk away from your employer or to help improve the organization from the inside. These decisions can be weighty, especially if, upon reflection, you find that the core of the product you work on, what your users are doing with it, or the business model itself, runs counter to your personal code. Thus, it can be helpful to learn about how other people, who confronted a similar question, responded and what happened next.

There are many lessons from people who share their stories publicly, but if examples of what you are grappling with personally do not surface, use this book to raise a conversation with trusted colleagues and mentors who may be able to discuss with you the dissonance you are experiencing. When I shared an early version of the ideas in this book with a group of designers from several different companies, this sentiment emerged particularly quickly: Participants said they wished they had a short book like this to give to their colleagues to start a conversation to raise the ethical bar.

TAKEAWAYS FROM THIS CHAPTER

» **Technique 18 of 20:** Develop a personal professional code of ethics, consisting of principles for your own behavior.
» **Technique 19 of 20:** Do ethnographic and diary research to fuel your passion for serving your users and, in the process, to gain a better understanding of your own role.
» **Technique 20 of 20:** Learn from others' self-reflection. Recognize that your role matters in delivering ethical products, but that often the best leadership is humble.

CONCLUSION

I have chosen breadth over depth in covering this enormous topic. I have beaten the drum of a general call-to-action louder than a detailed prescription to build ethical versions of specific types of products. This introductory book is intended for anyone currently involved in the product development process or who is a student of the process and would like to be involved in the future to improve the approach we are taking to plan, build, and deliver ethical products. This includes entrepreneurs, general managers, innovation leaders, product managers, UX designers, engineers, and legal "product" counselors.

If you've gotten to this point in the book, I would love for you to tell me who you are and how you think we should further raise the ethical bar. You may be part of a large company's "trust and safety" department, evaluating the propriety of content. You may be a data scientist developing predictive analytics or a recommendations engine. You may be a product manager trying to form specific habits in your users. You may be a UX designer, designing for people with disabilities. You may be an information security professional, whose competition has grappled with a security breach. You may be a salesperson or customer success professional who hears valuable input everyday about the ethical shortcomings of yours or your competitors' solutions.

These roles are just a small fraction of who you are and what you do. Together, we can dive much deeper for different audiences and I would love to do that in collaboration with you. If you'd like to confer with me to raise the ethical bar, please email me at *EthicalProductDevelopment@gmail.com*.

READING LIST

Reference material follows chapter sequence. For each of the 20 techniques listed as takeaways at the end of each chapter, I've put together "Resources to Consult" (i.e., go-to material for how to apply tactical concepts) and "Examples in Practice" (case studies of individuals, teams, and companies). You'll find the "Resources to Consult" below. For the "Examples in Practice," as well as complete reference material and commentary, please visit my public notebook: https://bit.ly/EthicalProductDevelopmentReadingListOneNote.

RESOURCES TO CONSULT

» **Technique 1 of 20**

> **Write a Product Code of Ethics (PCOE) to guide your work. Recognize that its power will be not only in its existence, but also in how it is applied to decision-making.**
>
> Schwab, Katharine. "2019 Is the Year to Stop Talking about Ethics and Start Taking Action." *Fast Company*, 4 Jan. 2019. https://www.fastcompany.com/90279512/2019-is-the-year-to-stop-talking-about-ethics-and-start-taking-action.

» **Technique 2 of 20**

> **Identify a champion for each of the PCOE principles, based on your colleagues' interest, expertise, and ability to engage with alternative points of view. Provide the champions with a playbook of activities to help the organization absorb, apply, and evolve the principles.**
>
> The Institute for the Future. https://ethicalos.org/. Accessed 31 May 2020.
> » Check out the Ethical OS toolkit to develop a risk-zone framework: Activity 1 of the Principle Playbook. Piloted by dozens of companies, the toolkit was developed by a think tank and an impact investment firm as the beginning of a movement toward encouraging start-ups to incorporate ethics into their innovation planning. The toolkit provides a strong, adaptable, starting point with three tools: The first is a set of concept scenarios ranging from

conversation bots to automation to prediction of "culture fit." The second tool lists eight risk zones of today, such as "economic and asset inequalities," "machine ethics and algorithmic bias," "data control and monetization," and "implicit trust and user understanding." You can consider a technology, product, or feature you are working on today and evaluate it against the risk zones. The third tool is a set of future-proofing strategies that can help a team begin to think about how to prevent harm over time.

Cavoukian, Ann. "Privacy By Design: The 7 Foundational Principles." Information and Privacy Commissioner of Ontario. Revised Jan. 2011. https://iapp.org/media/pdf/resource_center/Privacy%20by%20Design%20-%207%20Foundational%20Principles.pdf.
» To audit your product by principle, for example, privacy by design, you may benefit from looking at a variety of simplified principles initiated around the world.

"Summary of OpenMind Content." *OpenMind*. https://openmindplatform.org/wp-content/uploads/New-Content-Summary-Sources-No-Intro.docx.pdf. Accessed 31 May 2020.
» Activity 4 of the Principle Playbook is to learn how to discuss ethical options and values. My first recommended resource is Jonathan Haidt's OpenMind platform to learn how to discuss values in the workplace. Underlying belief systems drive much of our initial take on a decision; open, respectful, and constructive dialogue is essential. The OpenMind

platform provides exercise for you to do with your colleagues to lay the foundation for this type of dialogue.

"A Framework for Ethical Decision-Making." Markkula Center for Applied Ethics at Santa Clara University. https://www.scu.edu/media/ethics-center/ethical-decision-making/A-Framework-for-Ethical-Decision-Making.pdf 1 Aug. 2015.
» This resource unpacks five classic ethics approaches to help regular people (i.e., those who have not studied philosophy) consider ethical options as we use new technology to solve problems. The approaches are applicable to technology decision-making and are used by companies across Silicon Valley, including Google. They can be used to inform your PCOE as well as to help your team make everyday decisions. (I discuss this more at length in my public notebook: https://bit.ly/EthicalProductDevelopmentReadingListOneNote.)

» **Technique 3 of 20**

Use personas intentionally. Consider how your product is used by people and how to address use cases that fall outside of "mainstream" or "happy path" scenarios.

Meyer, Eric and Sara Wachter-Boettcher. *Design for Real Life*. A Book Apart, 2016.
» In this book, the authors urge product teams to use a number of inclusive design practices, such

as reframing definition of target users, to include those people who are using their solution in the messy conditions of life, whether in extreme or everyday stress.

Wachter-Boettcher, Sara. *Technically Wrong: Sexist Apps, Biased Algorithms, and Other Threats of Toxic Tech.* W.W. Norton & Company, Inc., 2017.

Kocsis, Anico. "User Personas: Traps and How to Overcome Them." *UXStudio,* 28 Aug. 2018, https://uxstudioteam.com/ux-blog/user-persona/
- » If you have mixed feelings about personas, as many do, this blog posts overviews the pitfalls and how to avoid them.

» **Technique 4 of 20**

Consider scale when you evaluate algorithmic solutions to user problems and apply O'Neil's four standards to avoid "mass destruction."

O'Neil, Cathy. *Weapons of Math Destruction: How Big Data Increases Inequality and Threatens Democracy.* Crown Publishing Group, 2016.

» **Technique 5 of 20**

It's worth developing a training workshop on the laws that govern your enterprise and the basic agreements between your company and your customers.

Go, Adrienne. "Product Counsel: How to Be THAT Kind of Lawyer." *LinkedIn*, 7 Oct. 2015, www.linkedin.com/pulse/product-counsel-how-kind-lawyer-adrienne-go.

"The Emerging Role of Product Counsel." *Axiom Law*, www.axiomlaw.com/blog/the-emerging-role-of-product-counsel. Accessed 31 May 2020.

» **Technique 6 of 20**

Look at the practices of companies within and outside of your industry to identify where your company may be falling short.

Davidson, Mike. "Superhuman Is Spying on You." *Mike Industries*, 2 July 2019, mikeindustries.com/blog/archive/2019/07/superhuman-is-spying-on-you.
» This post inspired a big portion of this book as well as the role of precedent in Chapter 3, but also sheds light on privacy norms.

» **Technique 7 of 20**

One of the most valuable future scenarios to play out is ethical crisis management, to equip your team to avoid a crisis in the first place or to respond effectively when one arises.

Luo, Hong, and Alberto Galasso. "The One Good Thing Caused by COVID-19: Innovation." *HBS Working Knowledge*, 7 May 2020, hbswk.hbs.edu/item/the-one-good-thing-caused-by-covid-19-innovation.

» **Technique 8 of 20**

To discover ethical solutions, you must raise ethical standards in both the desired results and the changes in behavior that would lead to them.

Seiden, Joshua. *Outcomes Over Output.* Sense & Respond Press, 2019.
» Seiden defines an outcome as a "change in behavior that drives business results." He encourages product teams to decompose the results they wish to see into actual changes in human behavior that have a high likelihood of leading to the result and then designing "experiments" around those actual observable changes in behavior and the quantifiable results. He identifies three "Magic Questions" to pinpoint the behavior changes and the results: (1) What are the user and customer behaviors that drive business results? (2) How can we get people to do more of these behaviors (e.g., through features, policy changes, promotions)?; (3) How do we know we're right?

» **Technique 9 of 20**

In the design phase, generate a large volume of high-ethics alternatives, using the Crazy Eights Method.

Knapp, Jake, et al. *Sprint: How to Solve Big Problems and Test New Ideas in Just Five Days*. 1st ed., Simon & Schuster, 2016, pp. 111–12.

» It may be difficult for your organization to pull off five-day design sprints exactly in the ways described in *Sprint*, yet most of the exercises, including the one I mention in the book about the Crazy Eights Method are extremely useful facilitation techniques to elicit yours and your team's best thinking as efficiently as possible, gaining momentum for progress.

» **Technique 10 of 20**

Once you have alternatives, use the Tarot Cards of Tech to ask questions of your alternatives.

"The Tarot Cards of Tech: The Power of Predicting Impact." *Artefact*, May 2018, www.artefactgroup.com/case-studies/the-tarot-cards-of-tech.

» The cards are printable!

» **Technique 11 of 20**

In finalizing alternatives to evaluate, develop hypothesis statements to design experiments to predict your odds of producing desired ethical outcomes.

Gothelf, Jeff. "Lean UX Canvas V2." *Jeff Gothelf*, 10 Sept. 2019, jeffgothelf.com/blog/leanuxcanvas-v2.
» The Lean UX Canvas can be used both in the design phase as well as in the build phase to enable the team to catalog the hypotheses and test risky assumptions. The results of the tests make great material for telling the story of how the feature evolved to its current state.

» **Technique 12 of 20**

Start your build phase *after* you have clarified the big picture through an internal press release.

Ladd, Brittain. "These Tools Are Why Amazon Is Successful." *Forbes*, 27 Aug. 2018, www.forbes.com/sites/brittainladd/2018/08/27/these-two-things-are-what-make-amazon-amazon/#7fd5450b5fd5.

"Ethics Explainer: What Is The Sunlight Test?" *The Ethics Centre*, 30 Aug. 2019, ethics.org.au/ethics-explainer-the-sunlight-test.

» **Technique 13 of 20**

In the build phase, formally document ethics requirements and decision-making through structured memos.

Bashaw, Ben. "How Jeff Bezos Turned Narrative into Amazon's Competitive Advantage." *Slab*, 5 Feb. 2019, https://slab.com/blog/jeff-bezos-writing-management-strategy/.

» **Technique 14 of 20**

In the test phase, incorporate ethics into internal quality assurance.

"Inspect and Adapt." *Scaled Agile Framework*, 8 Jan. 2020, www.scaledagileframework.com/inspect-and-adapt.

Smith, Randy. "5 Tips for Leading a Great Inspect & Adapt Workshop." *Icon Agility Services*, 22 May 2019, blog.iconagility.com/5-tips-for-leading-a-great-inspect-adapt-workshop.

» **Technique 15 of 20**

Incorporate ethics into alpha and beta testing.

"What Is Beta Testing? A Complete Guide." *Software Testing Help*, 16 Apr. 2020, www.softwaretestinghelp.com/beta-testing.

» **Technique 16 of 20**

> **Post-launch, see released features as the beginning of the work as opposed to the end. Apply a behavioral science-based approach to clarifying "promoting" and "inhibiting" pressures. This enables product teams to focus on driving outcomes ethically.**
>
> Saez, Andrea. "How to Build a Product Roadmap Everyone Understands." *ProdPad | Product Management Software*, 5 Sept. 2019, www.prodpad.com/blog/how-to-build-a-product-roadmap-everyone-understands.
>
> Wallaert, Matt. *Start at the End: How to Build Products that Create Change.* Portfolio/Penguin, 2019.

» **Technique 17 of 20**

> **Post-launch, engage in an ongoing in-app dialogue with your end users. This is a great way to stay committed to improving the ethical impact of your solution.**
>
> "In-App Survey Questions: Guidelines and Templates." *Instabug Blog*, 11 Oct. 2018, instabug.com/blog/in-app-survey-questions-templates.

» **Technique 18 of 20**

Develop a personal professional code of ethics, consisting of principles for your own behavior.

"How to Create Your Code of Ethics (with Examples)." *Indeed*, 12 Dec. 2019, https://www.indeed.com/career-advice/career-development/create-code-of-ethics.

Dutt, Radhika. "The Hippocratic Oath of Product Leadership." *ProductCraft by Pendo*, 3 Dec. 2019, productcraft.com/perspectives/the-hippocratic-oath-of-product-leadership.
» Dutt's "Radical Product Thinking" helps product leaders envision the change they want to create with their product, which is often tied to their underlying goals and values.

» **Technique 19 of 20**

Do ethnographic and diary research to fuel your passion for serving your users and, in the process, to gain a better understanding of your own role.

Roller, Margaret. "The Five Observer Roles in Ethnography." *Research Design Review*, 12 Nov. 2017, researchdesignreview.com/2017/10/19/the-five-observer-roles-in-ethnography.

"How to Do Diary Studies, a Great Alternative to Field Studies." *User Interviews*, www.userinterviews.com/ux-research-field-guide-chapter/diary-studies. Accessed 31 May 2020.

"UX Research Methods: Pros and Cons of Diary Studies." *Motivate Design*, 1 Mar. 2019, www.motivatedesign.com/ux-research-methods-pros-and-cons-of-diary-studies.

Hasley, Mac. "How to Conduct a Diary Study: A Start-to-Finish Guide." *Dscout*, dscout.com/people-nerds/diary-study-guide. Accessed 31 May 2020.

» **Technique 20 of 20**

Learn from others' self-reflection. Recognize that your role matters in delivering ethical products, but that often the best leadership is humble.

"Jim Collins—Concepts—Level 5 Leadership." *Jim Collins*, www.jimcollins.com/concepts/level-five-leadership.html. Accessed 31 May 2020.

"Jim Collins—Articles—Can You Grow into Level 5 Leadership." *Jim Collins*, www.jimcollins.com/article_topics/articles/can-you-grow-into-level-5.html#articletop. Accessed 31 May 2020.

ACKNOWLEDGMENTS

I want to recognize many of my thinker-doer colleagues at EAB, LexisNexis, and other companies who lead with conscience and embolden me to do the same. Of course, a forever thank you to my family, friends, and mentors who encouraged me to write this book, even though I have a semi-rational fear of internet trolls.

PAVANI REDDY is a product leader focused on developing ethical, effective solutions in education and information. Currently a leader of product management and user experience at EAB, Pavani is known for cultivating high-performing, creative, and ethical teams. She is passionate about practical, student-centered education for learners of all ages and stages. She holds an MBA and a law degree from the University of Virginia and a degree in economics from Brown University. When she's not at work, Pavani spends time with her daughter and husband and serves on the Board of Directors of The Positivity Project, a nonprofit focused on helping hundreds of K–12 schools to develop character strengths in their students.

ethicalproductdevelopment@gmail.com
pavanireddy1

Printed in Poland
by Amazon Fulfillment
Poland Sp. z o.o., Wrocław